DON'T DO IT—

WE LOVE YOU,

MY HEART

DON'T DO IT—
WE LOVE YOU,
MY HEART

POEMS

Jonathan Fink

DZANC
BOOKS

DZANC
BOOKS

2580 Craig Rd.
Ann Arbor, MI 48103
www.dzancbooks.org

First Edition: January 2025
Cover design by Matthew Revert
Interior design by Michelle Dotter

ISBN: 9781938603167

Printed in the United States of America

10 9 8 7 6 5 4 3 2 1

CONTENTS

DON'T DO IT—WE LOVE YOU, MY HEART   *09*

I.

GORBACHEV'S BIRTHMARK   *17*
AND WHO WILL COME FOR YOU?   *20*
CAT ON A HOT TIN ROOF   *30*
GRAVES   *32*

II.

A BRIEF HISTORY OF EXECUTION   *35*

III.

LEONARDO'S MISTAKE   *47*
QUINTA DEL SORDO   *51*
PROSPERITY GOSPELS   *54*
THE SUCCESSION OF MOTHERS   *56*
SOMETHING USEFUL   *60*
JOINED TO ALL THE LIVING THERE IS HOPE   *64*
A YEAR OF GROWTH   *73*

IV.

THE BIRTH OF VENUS   *81*

WHEN YOU LEAST EXPECT IT   *84*

PROXIMA CENTAURI   *86*

THE STORM ON THE SEA OF GALILEE   *89*

V.

THE LETTING DOWN   *97*

HOW TO FIGHT THE LION   *101*

A SHORT CONCEIT FOR LOSS   *104*

FOLLOWING MY DAUGHTER'S FITTING
    FOR A PROSTHETIC EYE   *105*

VI.

HOW ONE CHOOSES TO SEE   *111*

ABOUT THE AUTHOR

ACKNOWLEDGMENTS

For Julie, Sibley, Margaret, and Hazel

DON'T DO IT—
WE LOVE YOU, MY HEART

Julio De Leon is pedaling across the George Washington Bridge,
   his trim form, though sixty-one, leaning into the eastbound breeze

as tractor-trailers apply hydraulic brakes and shudder
   in between the honking cars, all twelve lanes of the upper level

stalled as Julio glides on the pedestrian path, the one artery
   unblocked from the city's heart where Julio works as a doorman

on the Upper West Side, having memorized the faces and names
   of the residents for whom with a gloved hand he has waved

down taxis or lifted packages from the trunk of a Town Car
   five days a week for the previous thirty-one years, the cartilage

in his knees ground down almost to bone so that now
   he must ride this route to and from work instead of run,

his body more attuned to nuance on the bike, the way the bridge
   trembles like a sheet of tin and sends vibrations through the frame

into his arms and legs, or how he sometimes parallels a flock of birds
   above the Hudson moving at his same velocity and height,

so close he used to sit up in the saddle, arms extended at his sides
  while steering with light gestures from his knees and hips,

a man in flight, at least until the day he fell, the front wheel
  catching on some unseen stone, the whole bike set

to wobble, his wife making him promise that night in their bed,
  after she'd dabbed his swollen lip, tweezered beads

of asphalt from his shoulder, that he would not carry on
  like this again, taking his hands from the bike or his eyes

from the path, *no matter what flies next to you*, his wife
  had said, knowing where to place the limits of her claim,

the wisdom of a long marriage, the two of them having raised
  their sons and a daughter, Julio himself the youngest of ten,

still the mischief-maker who winks at his wife over dinner prayers,
  over her faux-stern gaze, his right hand slipping the dog a strip

of pepper steak beneath the table, the dog's tail thumping
  the ground like Julio's wife's heart in her chest, the way her heart

still leaps each evening when she sees him coming up the drive,
  setting sun at his back, his body in eclipse, features taking

form as he slows into the shadow of the carport's awning,
  releases his toe clips, and swings his leg from the bike

in a singular motion, the same way, now halfway across
  the George Washington Bridge, he slows at the sight of a dog

leashed to the railing, Julio's bike shoes clicking on the asphalt
  when he lays the bike down, bends slowly to the small dog,

and rubs the dog's sternum to quiet its whimpering,
  Julio not looking down at the dog but ahead to the boy

just beyond the waist-high railing, the boy leaning
  out from the bridge like a carved figurehead on the prow

of a ship, the boy two hundred feet above the slate-gray chop
  of the Hudson, his T-shirt and striped shorts whipping

against his body like a sail in cross-cutting winds
  so that when the boy turns, his face beneath the baseball cap

visible to Julio for the first time, Julio opens his hands
  and steps slowly toward the boy, Julio working through

the scene's improbable calculus, the rush-hour jam
  of cars, the Port Authority officers who walk the bridge

for jumpers all now gone for the day, evening coming on,
  and though he does not scroll through numbers in his mind,

he knows them from the daily papers sold outside
  the building where he works, the voices on the sidewalk

rising with the news each day, or, worse, the silence after,
  the nothingness of how it seems the sky absorbs each jump,

the body disappearing in the air, though Julio, of course,
  knows that isn't true, that the earth pulls every form to it

indifferently, eight dead this year already, another forty saved
  by intervention, the papers say, the public calling for a barrier,

some kind of shield, the process stymied by facts and figures,
  actuarial will, prohibitive costs, even the danger the barrier

itself would pose, catching the wind like a sail and causing
   the deck to flex and jump, though Julio thinks of none of this

in the moment and instead searches for words to be a plank
   to the boy, *don't do it—we love you, my heart,* Julio will later tell

a reporter he said, Julio unsure, though, if this were the phrase,
   the spell gone, disappearing in the air the moment Julio moves,

the words a ribbon descending to the Hudson as Julio reaches
   for the boy, *in a second, only in a second,* his right arm curling

around the boy *like a shepherd's crook* the reporter will write,
   Julio unaware of the other man nearby on the bridge,

a bystander who snaps a photo of the boy beyond the rail
   before hurrying to Julio's side, Julio and the bystander pulling

the now-crying boy back across the rail together, Julio not letting go,
   talking to the boy, words to pin him to the path, the bridge,

though not words alone, Julio's arms encircling him,
   the boy not fighting Julio, but coiled, the urge to jump,

Julio believes, still incubating there, as the other man waves
   the traffic forward, the expressions of the drivers quizzical,

one woman rolling down the passenger window to point
   to the small dog tethered to the rail, the dog barking,

jerking at the leash, so that the man unties it and carries
   the dog to Julio and the boy, the two of them sitting upright,

Julio not letting go when the man sets the dog in the lap of the boy,
   and it places its paws on his chest, traffic parting for the cruiser

and ambulance pushing through as lights splash the bridge's cables
  and girders, both Julio and the boy looking up together to see

the faces of the EMTs, one woman bending to them, her hand
  on Julio's shoulder, instructing him to release the boy, Julio's fingers

intertwined and cramping, knotted roots that he shakes loose
  then stands, Julio already looking for his bike, his wife anxious

at home, how he knows that she will worry, his phone vibrating
  in the bike's cloth satchel as an officer waves Julio over

for a statement, the bystander showing the officer the photograph
  of the boy, all of them soon to be gone, dispersed like the ambulance

moving now from the bridge or the signal horn sounding below
  on the Hudson, a lone boat passing unseen in the dark.

I.

GORBACHEV'S BIRTHMARK

The coaches called it "dressing out," our transformation
  after lunch, four days a week (with art instead on Fridays)
into gray elastic-waistband shorts and V-neck shirts,
  our surnames stitched in neon orange two inches
to the right and three above the heart. We had seven minutes
  from the bell to find our seated places on the court,
and mine, in memory, was on the three-point line,
  not at the apex of the arc, but just beyond, the beginning
of the curve's descent. When one of us was late, unkempt,
  the coaches made us do an exercise called "squat-thrusts"
where we placed our hands against the floor
  and shot our feet behind us, brought them in, then leapt
into the air, our fingers spread in jazz hands
  (though the coaches never would have used that term)
as the thinnest coach, Coach Wayland, gave a lecture
  on the Russians, how we'd never beat them with our shoes
untied, and the oldest coach, Coach Day, counted down
  as if to launch, his face crimson as Gorbachev's birthmark.

These were the afternoons of shuttle runs and "suicides,"
  dodgeball, which the fattest coach called "murder ball"
while twirling a whistle, winding and unwinding
  its string around two fingers. We Greco-Roman wrestled
on a rollout mat, were drilled on ancient holds and moves:

the guillotine, the ankle pick, the arm bar and the barrel roll.
Outside of class, we mimicked Rowdy Roddy Piper's brogue
   and Jimmy "Superfly" Snuka's leaps, but inside the locker room
we neither preened nor primped, but steeled ourselves
   with faux solemnity for battle. "It's not the size of the dog
in the fight; it's the size of the fight in the dog," Coach Wayland,
   sitting backward on a metal folding chair, would say
as boys were weighed and partnered up, his right hand lifting
   to his bottom lip an empty soda can into which he'd spit
tobacco juice then wipe his mouth on the back of his arm.

The coaches often paired me (I was wiry, fast)
with a heavy, slower boy, and as I slipped and moved,
   evaded and rejoined, they called out instructions
("reversal," "roll," "lock the leg") until the other boy
   would sometimes quit, his asthma winning out,
or he would trap me under him with more of a flop
   than a practiced move as Coach Day, on hands
and knees, hovered his palm above the mat to strike it
   the moment both my shoulders came to rest.

It's tempting, though inaccurate, to believe that what
   the coaches tried to teach us was acceptance of surrender,
what the Baptist preachers in our small town might have claimed
   to be the hand of God descending, or Jacob grappling with the angel.
"You think the Ruskies give up so easy?" Coach Wayland,
   bending down beside us on the mat, whispered in our ears.
He called us "milksops" and "gutless wonders,"
   and though I knew these men had wives and kids
(I once congratulated the fattest coach on a newborn son,
   a fact I'd learned because my mother labored with his wife
in the public schools; bemused, he'd scratched his head
   and studied me and almost smiled), still it was hard
to imagine they ever left the gym, the locker room,

rather that, like cosmonauts, they perpetually orbited its atmosphere,
inhospitable as deep space, all sweat and cheap cologne.

By the time the Berlin Wall came down, we'd moved on
to badminton, a juggling unit, lawn bowling on the soccer field.
Promotion to the high school loomed, and as winter
turned to spring, my peers and I abandoned Wayland,
Day, and left them barking orders in our wake.
"Old soldiers never die; they just fade away," MacArthur said,
    which we did, pleasantly, to trigonometry and tennis,
then college, jobs, families. And as the coaches faded
    to administrative positions or to history classrooms
when budget cuts to gym descended, the great threats of which
    Coach Day and Wayland warned never entered in our lives.
Instead, older now than they were then, I find an eagerness
    that rises in the long, dull slog of middle age to push aside
the boardroom table, mid-PowerPoint, and take my colleague Jones
    or Johnson in a figure-four or hammerlock, perhaps a hip throw
in a Brooks Brothers suit. "What the hell are you waiting for?"
    Coach Day will whisper in my ear. "I'll explain it
to the boss," Coach Wayland answers. "Comrades," I'll say
    to Johnson and Jones as they remove their jackets and start
to circle the makeshift mat, "you have but one life to live.
Be vigilant. Be bold. At the whistle, begin."

AND WHO WILL COME FOR YOU?

What purer way could we descend than drunk
on Pabst Blue Ribbon beer, our battered trucks
and cars (most hand-me-downs from parents
or—the case of one or two—from siblings gone
into the Army or to jail) lined on the shoulder

of a gravel road, all headlights off and music silenced,
as we gathered at a spot that looked no different
than the pastureland surrounding us for twenty miles?
It took you numbnuts long enough, a football player
said and threw an empty can into the field

before he jumped down from his pickup's hood.
Two girls climbed from the cab. One carried half
a six-pack by the empty rings (it dangled to her knees,
the cans like fish along a stringer) as the other girl
took three steps, teetered in her heels, then laughed—

a snort—and held onto the left side mirror of the truck.
Already buzzed before we left her house,
I'd come here with the one girl I believed
I'd ever love. Inside my car, she'd rolled
the window down, slid off her shoes, and placed

her bare feet on the dash, her forearms drawing knees
to chest as her hair moved with the patterns of the breeze.
In the field, the football player pressed his boot
down on the bottom wire of a barbed-wire fence
while with his hand he drew the middle wire

upward, tense, as if it were a compound bow.
My girlfriend crawled through first, then I,
then all the other students, mostly cheerleaders
and jocks, although a roper who'd arrived alone
(he cultivated friendships with the jocks because,

like them, he liked to fight with strangers)
pulled his cowboy hat down tighter on his head
and slipped beneath the middle wire.
I helped the football player, last one through,
then joined the others where they whispered loudly

in the field. The only light came from the moon,
and in the field my girlfriend's skin was like the color
of the gravestones in the cemetery that I passed
each day driving back and forth from school.
As I stood before a slab of poured cement

about the size of three adjacent tennis courts,
a seam dividing it in half, I thought, *The gates of hell
are open night and day* (a line from Dante I had come across
two months before when reading for a class report—
the topic we'd been given was "The Consequence of Sin").

My girlfriend cinched one arm around a rusted metal rung
preceding other rusted metal rungs that formed a ladder
going downward in a concrete cylinder beneath a grating,
eight feet wide, the hatch tipped back and resting

on the lock the football players had "released"

with bolt cutters, a crowbar. When I reached the bottom
of the cylinder my girlfriend took my arm and placed
the flashlight in my hand. She shivered and I lay
my coat across her shoulders as we stepped into a room
(the door was like a submarine hatch on its side,

but larger, six feet in diameter, the screw heads big
as fists that held the hinges to the wall). Inside the room
were metal bunks along two walls, three consoles
with black monitors, and empty rectangles in metal tabletops
that once held keypads or remote controls,

now sprouting wires and severed cables.
Someone yelled *hello* from just beyond us
through the second door, the word resounding
as we stepped from the control room to the silo
where the missile once was housed—a cylinder of darkness,

air, approximately fifty feet across, and rimmed
by metal grating (platforms ten feet wide encircling every floor)
and ladders that had given workers access to each section
of the missile. When the roper tossed a metal cabinet door
he'd jimmied loose into the darkness at the center of the silo,

we all waited for the sound of metal crashing
to the concrete floor. Instead, we heard a splash.
I lay down on my belly at the grating's edge
and shined my flashlight to the bottom of the silo
where the water's surface rippled eighty feet or so

below us. *Rainwater,* I said, *the bottom must not drain,*
as a cheerleader unzipped the football player's backpack

and removed five cans of spray paint, handing them
to other cheerleaders and jocks before they sprayed
their initials beside the others on the silo's walls.

I gathered myself up and went to join my girlfriend
where she waited back in the control room.
Sitting on a bunk, she raised a finger to her lips
the moment I entered as she pointed
to the drunk girl who had almost fallen

from the ladder while descending, now asleep
and snoring softly in a metal chair spot welded
to the floor before a console in the middle of the room.
My girlfriend slid her other hand beneath my shirt,
her palm against my chest, and whispered

something in my ear I couldn't fully understand
(the words were indistinct, the way one speaks
when waking or just falling into sleep). Her breath
smelled like a mix of cigarettes and alcohol—a smell
inseparable from her, so strong that even now

the slightest scent of smoke (a stranger stepping
into an elevator or the hint of cigarettes that lingers
in a rental car or hotel room) transports me to her home,
her bedroom where she'd lie on top of me;
her stomach muscles tightened slightly

when she spoke, and I would feel their movement
in my own. Her parents never came to check on us.
No father, speaking loudly, made his way downstairs.
No mother brought a plate of cookies to her daughter's room.
My girlfriend told me once of how her father

(not the man her mother met ten years ago—
the man her mother married quickly who sold insurance
and wore a bolo tie, who, nervous, sucked his mustache
with his lower lip while staring at the ceiling—
but her *father* father: drunk extraordinaire, the man

her mother never spoke about) had called my girlfriend
(she was nine years old) into the living room, her mother
not yet home from work (her mother was a nursing
student then) and, sitting on their broken futon,
lined a row of bullets one by one by one along the surface

of the coffee table as he told her that he needed
her to bring her mother to the living room. He raised
a pistol from the coffee table when he told my girlfriend this
and spun the cylinder. She said she waited for her mother,
watching for her through the storm door's glass,

and when my girlfriend saw her mother pull into the drive,
she stepped outside and ran to meet her mother's car.
My girlfriend told the story frankly, never changing in her tone:
I led her to the house and closed the door behind her.
When my mother did return (it felt like half an hour, though

it probably wasn't more than six or seven minutes from the moment
when she stepped inside), no suitcase in her hand,
just walking quickly, it was then when I began to cry.
She lifted me from where I sat beside the door
and carried me, my mother never speaking, to the car.

My girlfriend said what she remembered most was standing
in the yard (a rock bed spreading from curb to house,
the duplex owners skeptical that renters cared enough
to mow a lawn) and how she knew she would have to follow

afterward whichever parent came back out. *My mother met*

my stepfather soon after that and moved us in his house.
Midwinter, four years later, when the stove went dead,
a new one had to be delivered and installed. My stepfather
was gone when it arrived, and as my mother signed
the paperwork the driver gave to her, another man

walked backward slowly, pulling on the dolly.
When my mother held the door for him he grunted
as a way of saying thanks. He didn't even look up.
"I think your father's in the kitchen working
on our stove," was what my mother said as I peered

from the den. We both hid in a bedroom as they finished.
When my father took the dolly to the truck, my mother called
into the den that she was busy in the other room—the men
should leave the way they came in. I watched my father
through the bedroom window as he waited in the truck.

He pulled the visor down and with the backside of his hand
he jiggled slightly up and down the skin beneath his chin.
It was the last time that I saw him. After that, we moved
down here. When lying on her bed, I asked my girlfriend
if she ever asked her mother what went on inside the house,

what happened with the bullets and the gun. She said
she didn't want to know, then turned her gaze away from me,
her cheek against my chest. I shivered as she worked
her fingers downward to my ribs and belly, and I closed my eyes.
Perhaps what I loved most about her was the fact she never

seemed to be fully at ease—not skittish, but removed;
in class, I'd catch her staring at the clock when other students

had their heads bent to a test, and when I picked her up three
days a week from diving practice after school, she'd always
be the first one from the building. Walking fast, her wet hair

drawn into a ponytail, she'd slide into the car and pull
the shoulder strap across her, snap the buckle closed,
while her teammates lingered in the locker room.
At meets, she sat alone, one towel at her waist,
her knees to chest, another towel on her shoulders.

Always, in between her dives, she placed her headphones
to her ears and drew the towel upward from her shoulders
to her head and let the towel settle over her until
the diving coach reached out and touched her on the shoulder,
signaling the time had come to dive. In air, my girlfriend's arms

and head would lead her body, and she tucked her head
against her knees when spinning forward, breaking
from her tuck, releasing in a flash, a spring uncoiled,
her body rigid as she sliced into the water. Once or twice
a meet she'd nail a dive—the perfect entry where the water

did not splash, but *ripped* (the phrase her coach would use),
receiving her without condition. Always in my memory
she is climbing slowly from the pool, her hands on each side
of the ladder, as she looks to see the scores the judges lift
(the plastic numbers, folding placards) just above their heads,

the same look (distant, quizzical) she gave beside me
in the bunker of the missile silo when we heard the steps
of other people coming down the ladder, heard their voices
(angry, clipped), and with the voices came the light:
four beams, intense and circling at the bottom of the ladder.

Both drunk cheerleaders were sleeping peacefully by then
and I assumed the jocks, the roper, and the other girls
had started smoking pot, their spray cans emptied, thrown
into the water at the bottom of the shaft. My girlfriend sat up
in the bunk beside me. When she looked at me with something

not too far removed from terror in her gaze, I thought,
Perhaps it is the workers from the silo, gone from here
for twenty years, or maybe it's the Russians come at last
(in homeroom, we had watched the movie seven times
where Communist commandos swarmed a lone

Midwestern high school, killing all inhabitants except
the students who resisted). Though I did not think it at the time,
perhaps my girlfriend thought the stranger coming down
the ladder was her father, that he'd found her once again.
But when I saw the first cop's boots and legs descending

into view, I knew the rancher must have seen our row
of cars, or heard us in the field, or, tired of students
sneaking onto his land, he'd waited up that Saturday
until we all descended, no way out, into the silo.
When the first cop stepped into the room he turned his light

on us. Removal went like this: the cheerleaders, the roper
and the jocks were searched beside us at the bottom
of the ladder just before we had to climb out one by one.
The cheerleaders and jocks had thrown their joints
into the darkness at the center of the silo when they heard

the cops call out, but soon the cops removed a Ziploc bag
of weed from the roper (he had brought it on request—
the other reason the jocks hung out with him).
The drunk girls both had woken up and blearily

they asked a cop to drive them home. And though

the officers all hardly spoke (they cuffed us
in the field before they led us to the cars), the rancher
would not stop. He asked our names. He told the cops
about the type of feed the cows would eat, the way
his wife had overcooked his food for thirty years

and how she'd died two years before. He'd found her
when he came in from the fields one night, spaghetti sauce
still bubbling on the stove, her hands in lap, her back against
a cabinet as she sat unmoving on the kitchen floor. He led us
to the gate, across the cattle guard and up the road until we stood

beside our vehicles, now flanked by several squad cars.
When the cops asked what the rancher wanted
them to do, he squinted, then he looked down at the ground.
One football player had been crying as we walked,
and when he heard the hesitation in the rancher's voice

he stopped his blubbering. *I got a blowtorch in the barn,*
the farmer said. *I should have welded shut that hatch before.*
The cops undid our handcuffs, and we rubbed our wrists.
We held our hands before us, staring at the fronts and backs.
The roper, cursing still, was escorted into a squad car.

They would kindly follow us until we reached the highway,
one cop said. *And then,* he snarled, *you're on your own.*
And when we pulled onto the highway and the cops turned back,
and other cars and trucks of friends took exits one by one,
I did not think of mercy or of luck or of fate. I only listened

to my girlfriend breathing softly in her sleep, her jacket
folded as a pillow and then wedged between the headrest

and the window. When we slowed before her house, I touched
her lightly on the arm to wake her. Memory is a type of dream,
I think. She looked at me and did not speak. She put her fingers

to my lips, a gesture I have never fully understood, the darkness
thinning through the car, the street, beyond the rows
and rows of homes. A robin swooped behind us, flashing
in the rearview mirror just before he settled on a power line.
Look, I said, but when she turned to find him, he was gone.

CAT ON A HOT TIN ROOF

"You can be young without money, but you can't be old without it,"
  Maggie the Cat admonishes Brick, moving in her slip

across the screen of the renovated theater in the West Texas town
  of my youth, a projector casting slow-moving clouds

onto the curved ceiling where the bulbs of small stars blink
  and flicker, though this showing is a Saturday matinee,

and the heat of mid-July just beyond the theater's doors rises
  in waves from the asphalt, thrums through the air

like desperation itself, the way the ranch hands and roughnecks,
  out of work because of drought or oil wells sunk

through caprock into barren earth, stand, hat in hand,
  beneath the awning of the post office, sweat dried

to a poor man's halo behind leather and silver-Concho-adorned
  hatbands, purchased by their wives or girlfriends

on a honeymoon or liaison in San Antonio while the entire time
  each man only thought of work, how, once spent, he stood

half naked at a hotel window overlooking the river winding
  its way through downtown, past shops and restaurants,

a mariachi band circling the tables for tips, the musicians
  moving like a river, the songs like a river, *No Tengo Dinero,*

El Rey, Volver, Volver, played over and over each night,
  as the ranch hand or roughneck ran his fingers through

his thinning hair then lifted the new hatband from a bedside table,
  the hatband he knew his wife or girlfriend could not afford,

traced his thumb along the edge of a Concho as if it were
  a Spanish coin dropped by Cabeza de Vaca on the banks

of the river, and though the roughneck or ranch hand
  did not speak—the silence in the room heavy as the humid air

in which the woman dozed—he thought some version
  of the mariachi's words, of the words *with money,* the word *young,*

that Maggie the Cat is trilling at Brick, her voice trembling
  like the drink in his hand—"you've got to be one or the other..."

GRAVES

No one would choose this earth for his home—
   the parched dirt tempered by drought,

mesquites rooted as teeth from unremitting wind.
   The headstones here lie flush to the ground,

all vases inverted and sheathed in stone.
   My mother has removed her heels and stands

above her father's grave. With stocking toe she marks
   the plots where I, my father and brother will lie.

Think of the nothing all prophets have claimed,
   dust from dust, a grain of sand. At rapture, this field

will be a stubborn pry—our hair and nails rooting
   even in death, without rain or air, provision or light.

II.

A BRIEF HISTORY OF EXECUTION

1.

Written in 1772 BC, the Code of Hammurabi contains the earliest known laws for justifiable execution.

2.

For example, if a man accuses another man of an injustice, the accused man will be plunged into a river, and, if innocent, he will rise to the river's surface. Conversely, unseen hands will draw him, if guilty, to the silt and darkness of the river bottom. Should the man reach the river's shore, the accuser will be put to death, and all he owns will be forfeited to the innocent man.

3.

Lex talionis, the law of retaliation, undergirds Hammurabi's Code: "If a man put out the eye of another man, his eye shall be put out."

4.

Deuteronomy, the fifth book of the Hebrew Bible, also advocates for *lex talionis*.

5.

Christ advocated for the law of forgiveness, as did Gandhi, and Martin Luther King.

6.

Mid-execution, Christ called out, "Father, forgive them, they know not what they do."

7.

The word "excruciating" derives from the Latin word "excruciates," meaning "out of the cross."

8.

When Narayan Godse, Gandhi's assassin, was executed by hanging in 1949, Gandhi's two sons pleaded unsuccessfully for Godse's life to be spared.

9.

King's assassin, James Earl Ray, evaded execution with a guilty plea, which he later attempted to recant, and then died in prison from complications of hepatitis C.

10.

Robert Kennedy, when telling a gathered crowd in Indianapolis of King's death, read aloud a poem by Aeschylus.

11.

From a podium erected on a flatbed truck, Robert Kennedy stayed the swelling anger of the crowd: *Even in our sleep, pain which cannot forget, falls drop by drop upon the heart...*

12.

His own assassin, Sirhan Sirhan, was sentenced to death, but the sentence was commuted to life in prison when the California Supreme Court invalidated all pending death sentences in 1972.

13.

As bodyguards and crowd members attempted to subdue Sirhan Sirhan, a seventeen-year-old busboy named Juan Romero cradled Robert Kennedy's head and placed a rosary in Kennedy's palm.

14.

When Robert Kennedy addressed the crowd in Indianapolis, he spoke in public for the first time about his brother's assassination.

15.

Five years prior, while his dog Sheba waited in the car, Jack Ruby, on national television, executed Lee Harvey Oswald with a snub-nosed Colt .38 revolver.

16.

Sentenced to death and awaiting a new trial, Jack Ruby was executed by pulmonary embolism brought on by lung cancer. Ruby and Oswald both died at Parkland Hospital, the same hospital at which John F. Kennedy had been pronounced dead.

17.

Jacqueline Kennedy introduced Robert Kennedy to Aeschylus' writing when he was grieving the death of his brother.

18.

Aeschylus, the father of tragedy, believed that knowledge arises from suffering.

19.

In his plays, Aeschylus executes character after character. Even Cassandra, whose ears were licked clean by snakes in Apollo's temple so that she might hear the future, could not escape her execution by Clytemnestra.

20.

In 456 BC, Aeschylus himself, the legend claims, was executed when an eagle dropped a tortoise from the sky.

21.

Animals figure prominently in execution lore.

22.

In the Twelve Tablets of the Roman Law, the crime of patricide called for the condemned to be drowned inside a sack that also contained a dog, a rooster, a viper, and an ape.

23.

In an execution for sport, three hotel owners in Niagara, New York, in 1827, obtained a condemned schooner, decorated it as a pirate ship, filled it with animals, and sent it over Horseshoe Falls to the delight of 15,000 spectators.

24.

The boat (the *Michigan*) was supposed to contain "animals of the most ferocious kind, such as panthers, wild cats and wolves," yet when the boat went over the falls, it contained only a buffalo, two raccoons, a dog, and a goose.

25.

In 1903, Thomas Edison, in an execution for business, electrocuted Topsy, a twenty-eight-year-old elephant from Coney Island's Luna Park. The execution was sanctioned because Topsy had killed three men over the previous three years.

26.

J.F. Blount, one of Topsy's keepers, had tried to feed her a lit cigarette, and she lifted him with her trunk and dashed him on the ground.

27.

Hanging had been considered as a means of execution for Topsy, but Edison stepped in and suggested electrocution by alternating current. To alert the public of the current's danger, Edison insisted that the execution be filmed.

28.

George Westinghouse, Edison's chief competitor, championed alternating current. Edison championed direct current.

29.

To guarantee Topsy's execution, Topsy was fed carrots laced with cyanide.

30.

One newspaper reported, "The execution was witnessed by 1,500 or more curious persons, who went down to the island to see the end of the huge beast, to whom they had fed peanuts and cakes in summers that are gone…"

31.

When Edison's stunt couldn't impede the rise of alternating current, Edison advocated for its use in the electric chair. He even tried to make Westinghouse's name into a verb. To Edison, death by electric chair meant getting "Westinghoused."

32.

In 1890, the first execution by electric chair was less than a rousing success.

33.

William Kemmler, a citizen of Buffalo, New York, who killed his common-law wife with a hatchet, received 1,000 volts for seventeen seconds. When the doctors noticed that Kemmler was still breathing, they increased the voltage to 2,000 volts. Blood vessels ruptured under his skin, and the stench of singeing hair filled the chamber.

34.

When he heard of the debacle, George Westinghouse said, without irony, "They would have done better using an ax."

35.

The word "electrocution" initially only referred to intentional execution by electricity, but soon encompassed accidental death by electricity as well.

36.

"Old Sparky," the electric chair at Sing Sing prison, was used in all executions in New York State from 1914 to 1963.

37.

Willie Francis, in 1946, became the first person to survive the electric chair.

38.

An intoxicated prison guard in Angola, Louisiana, incorrectly installed a portable electric chair named "Gruesome Gertie." When the switch was thrown, Willie Francis allegedly yelled, "Take it off! Let me breathe!"

39.

His case went to the Supreme Court, and his lawyers argued that even though Willie Frances did not die, he had, in fact, been executed.

40.

The Supreme Court was not persuaded, and Willie Francis was re-executed successfully in 1947.

41.

Yet there have been successful escapes.

42.

Back in Niagara, New York, before the *Michigan* went over Horseshoe Falls, two small bears that had been placed on the boat leapt into the Niagara River and swam to Goat Island when the *Michigan* began to tear apart in the rapids.

43.

Rescued downriver after going over the falls, the goose also survived.

44.

In 1915, Wenceslao Moguel survived nine shots from a firing squad during the Mexican Revolution. Presumed dead, he waited until the solders left and then crawled to safety, making a business from his mangled face and touring the country for the second half of his life.

45.

To conclude, there is this: If knowledge rises from suffering, what is to be made of Frano Selak?

46.

Frano Selak: the Croatian music teacher who escaped death seven times, who survived a train crash into an icy river, a fall from a plane when he landed in a haystack, a bus crash, two car crashes (one of which burned away all of his hair when fuel spewed from the air vents), being knocked down by a van, and, lastly, having his car hit by a United Nations bus as he turned a corner on a mountain road, catapulting him to the canopy of a tree as his car exploded below him on the mountainside.

47.

In 2006, Frano won one million dollars with a lottery ticket he bought in celebration of his fifth wedding.

48.

The ticket was the first he had ever purchased.

49.

In an interview, he said he was the happiest he had been in his life. He said, "All I need at my age is my Katarina. Money would not change anything."

50.

He donated most of the winnings to charity and relatives, setting aside funds only for his hip replacement and to build a shrine for St. Mary, whom he viewed as the mother of all, whose own son, like Frano, had demonstrated power over the grave.

III.

LEONARDO'S MISTAKE

Tonight, as the last light falls across
    the dining room table, across the remains
        of the meal my wife Julie and I have yet

to clear, our young daughters finished
    and excused to play upstairs as Julie dabs
        the last piece of baguette onto the small plate

of olive oil and balsamic, the contours
    of her face in the candlelight reminding
        me of the Apostle John in *The Last Supper,*

his countenance calm among the twelve
    gathered disciples, all held in the moment
        Christ has said, "One of you shall betray me,"

John leaning away from the words,
    his gaze turned downward, thoughts
        mysterious as the curve of his closed

mouth, Peter whispering to him,
    one hand placed on John's collarbone,
        the other holding a knife, a reference

by Leonardo to Peter soon to cut off
        the ear of the high priest's servant
                when soldiers arrive to take Christ

away, only the gospel of Luke relaying
        that Christ healed the wound, saying,
                "Suffer ye thus far," the gospel unclear

as to whether Christ touched the side
        of the servant's head or restored
                the severed ear gently like a fallen bird

to its nest, the gesture not unlike the touch
        of my wife when I am lost in thought
                or memory, her hand at my cheek

directing me back to the present
        like the brush of a fingertip across
                still water, the reflection rippling,

retrieving me as she does now, placing
        her hand on mine, and I relay to her
                what I heard today on the car radio

as I circled the neighborhood, trying
        to get Margaret to nap, a psychologist
                speaking about time, his hypothesis

being that there is no present,
        that every moment is only the past
                or the future, separated, he said,

like the line an ocean makes on a shore,
        every experience approaching or gone,
                either the light of an oncoming train

or the sound of its whistle fading after,
        "So how would he account for art?"
                my wife asks, my wife for whom the language

of "composition" and "line" are visual terms,
        which she illustrated early in our dating,
                having just arrived from a studio class,

opening her portfolio on my kitchen table
        and turning through one large sheet
                after another of charcoal and line

faces and forms, how she would sit me
        across from her as a subject as well,
                rising at times to tilt and still my head

for the light, her hands instructive
        like a barber's hands before she'd return
                to her chair, gazing both at me and beyond,

not unlike, I think now, Leonardo in Milan
        taking more than a year to find his models
                for Judas and Christ, indifferent to his patron

and time, which is also the point my wife
        makes about art, its unwavering present,
                Christ's words forever holding in the air

even as the painting itself fissures,
>   Leonardo forgoing established technique
>>   and painting directly onto the dry walls

of Santa Maria delle Grazie, very little
>   of his original fresco remaining,
>>   its form having been tinkered with

for five hundred years, surviving bombings
>   in the Second World War, botched restorations,
>>   the cutting of a door through Christ's feet

in the rectory wall, even the conversion
>   of the room to a stable by Napoleon's troops,
>>   those soldiers, too, silent at first beneath

Christ's outstretched hands, before one
>   of them, weary from marching, from war,
>>   called out for something to eat and to drink.

QUINTA DEL SORDO

I wish that I could find myself asleep tonight
        in a house on the banks of the Manzanares,
                the river that begins in the Sierra de Guadarrama

and flows through Madrid before joining
        the Jarama, the Tagus, and then emptying
                four hundred miles away into the Atlantic,

the house christened Quinta del Sordo,
        The Villa of the Deaf Man, so named for the owner
                who, in silence, walked its grounds

during the Spanish uprising of 1808
        and the Peninsula War, selling the home
                to the artist Goya in 1819, who, deaf himself,

began to paint directly on the plaster walls,
        only his maid and lover, Leocadia Weiss,
                accompanying him, her dark hair veiled

in Goya's painting, one of the last
        of the sequence throughout the home,
                the elder Goya rumored to be mad

at seventy-two, resigning to the country
        from the court in Madrid, the river cutting
                the countryside like a slash from a French bayonet,

and Goya's hand rising to the plaster walls,
        his brush tip wet with oils as Leocadia
                poses in a funereal dress, Goya placing her

in the painting beside what is believed to be
        a burial mound, and though I do not know
                what I would dream there in that home,

I would like for Goya's dog to guide me,
        the dog of whom only his black muzzle
                and head are seen rising above the ochre earth

that divides his painting horizontally in two,
        the context unknown as to whether the dog
                is sinking into the earth or raising his head

cautiously from his den, and I imagine him
        nudging me, asleep in the lone bed centered
                in the upstairs room, the dog, not tripping

over his paws or shaking his coat, but placing
        his chin on my thigh with the same pressure
                with which someone might wake a child,

or lower the barrel of an adversary's gun,
        and without a whimper the dog would lead me
                past each painting, past *Saturn Devouring His Son,*

past *The Fates, Two Women and a Man,*
      past *Fight with Cudgels,* the background
            of all the paintings a kind of mottled gray,

less dark than the dog's sleek fur, wet from a swim
      perhaps, his coat dark as the night sky, made darker
            by the piercing of stars, their pinprick light falling

on the Manzanares, on the banks of which
      the dog and I stand, his pearlescent eyes round
            as the moon glinting on the river's wet sand.

THE PROSPERITY GOSPELS

"If your son asked for bread, would you give him
  a stone?" a televangelist, in front of a ten-foot-wide

gold rotating globe, the curls of his gelled hair
  held firm as the waves of the Red Sea, implores

his congregation and the viewers at home,
  not, he insists, for their money, but instead,

in an arena no less in size than the Roman Colosseum,
  for their *abundance*, the camera searching

the crowd at the word, finding even the faces
  of those who seem unsure, their lives

resembling, in most ways, my own, I imagine
  from the downstairs couch of my split-level home,

a spot less than a pinprick on the curve of the earth,
  less than the breath of my infant daughter asleep

in my arms, her mother and sisters dozing upstairs,
  our home's only light the television's glow that frames

both me and our newest born, a home full of children
   asleep being *more quiet than an empty house,*

a comedian once said, the quietude, I believe,
   that Christ often sought, at least the Christ who seems

most human to me, who requested a boat for relief
   from the crowds and grew tired the way all people tire,

who said, *the poor you will always have with you,*
   but you will not always have me, a perplexing statement

to be sure, at least more so than *the first shall be last,*
   and the last shall be first, the virtue all parents attempt

to instill, though, I admit, with middling success,
   my own children still lurching for bread at dinner

each night, litigating their allotments in this and all things,
   which is perhaps why the evangelist says *abundance*

again to the crowd's applause, the word held
   like the Host itself on their lips as the news program

cuts to the more recent past and a clip of flooding
   in the evangelist's town, a journalist wading

through water waist deep to speak to the homeless
   displaced by the storm, behind them the empty arena

sealed tight as a tomb, cordoned off from those
   in need in exactly the way I feared most as a child,

that the heart, on a whim, could be hardened to stone,
   whether King or Pharaoh, my loved ones, or me.

THE SUCCESSION OF MOTHERS

"Take this," a man resembling,
          from a distance, my long-dead grandfather
                    bellowed on the corner of Boylston

and Tremont, his breath holding
          on the winter air like exhaust
                    from the smokestacks and chimneys

I observed each day, turn of a new century,
          through the graffitied windows
                    of an Orange Line subway car

that trembled and shook
          from Sullivan Square to my Chinatown stop,
                    the man's middle finger sprung

like a switchblade at protestors
          on the opposite curb as he stammered,
                    "and send it to ya motha!"

his other hand holding fast
          to the ball end of a weathered cane,
                    the city in turmoil, though I do not recall

now with which sides the individuals
        aligned, only that some of the protestors
                glared at the man and others laughed,

most likely at his impotent rage
        or the thought, literal, of his photograph
                arriving in their mother's mail,

his voice recorded on a cassette tape
        turned back and forth in the gray light
                of Medford or Charlestown, the first package

these mothers had received in months
        or even years from children long grown
                and lost to the world, or so the mothers

had thought, one mother in this succession
        of mothers receiving, in my imagination,
                the man's actual finger, not severed

or taken by force, but surrendered
        to the crowd through which he passed,
                the finger slipped from the man's hand

like the magic trick all fathers employ,
        the finger disappearing in the moment
                and not returned, destined or cursed

to travel from home to home,
        like the duffle bag, all fuchsia and turquoise,
                that my wife and her family received

for one week each year when she was a child,
        the bag containing a statute of Our Lady of Fatima,
                arriving, or so I choose to believe, on their porch

in a flurry of wind and with a sound like a knock
        at the door, though they couldn't be sure,
                and what else could they do but take her in,

my wife and her sisters attending, placing
        the statue on their cleared foyer table,
                unpacking and positioning her crown, her hands

extended in welcome, revealing her pierced
        and thorn-encircled heart, its sacred form
                capped with fire and emanating brushstrokes

of light, like the image of the sun spinning
        in the sky on the VHS tape that came in the bag,
                the image my wife says she remembers most,

as well as the story her school's nuns told
        of the apparition of Our Lady of Fatima appearing
                to Pope John Paul II as he lay bleeding

in St. Peter's Square, having been shot four times
        by an attempted assassin, the Pope insisting
                afterward that the Blessed Mother redirected

the bullets away from his heart, a belief
        he held so strongly that, when recovered,
                he sought out her shrine and placed

one of the four bullets in her statue's crown,
      the bullet the size of a fingertip
         and clean though having passed

through the meat of a man, a gift
      I know from which I would recoil,
         though what is a statute if not composed,

no different from those same mothers
      who, each evening after Mass, still light
         a candle in their shades-drawn homes

and say the Rosary for a wayward child,
      their hands traversing from bead to bead,
         reciting the prayers their own mothers prayed.

SOMETHING USEFUL

When the sound returns, faint at first,
      more pulse than pitch, my wife's left hand
            on my chest, not shaking me awake,

but still as a ship at sea, becalmed
      on my heart without wind or waves,
            I do not hesitate, but rise, already dressed

in shirt and shorts, and shuffle downstairs,
      scooping the neighbor's key from the foyer
            table just as I have the previous two times

tonight, the moon, not so much rising
      in the sky but passing among the tops
            of the pines, as if it too were peering out

to find the source of the shrieking bird,
      my neighbors gone for a month for the late
            marriage of their youngest son, asking

my wife and me to keep an eye on things,
      none of us expecting the faulty alarm,
            unfixable until Monday, and wailing

every four hours, reminding me,
    in a small way, of my daughters
        as newborns and those first fitful months,

my wife waking again and again as I do
    tonight, though an alarm of course
        is also not like a newborn at all,

a newborn needing to be nursed
    and consoled, to be sung to and held,
        just as anger, Buddhist monks believe,

needs to be soothed when it wakes
    like a crying child, though I don't feel
        anger tonight, crossing the street

to my neighbor's home, only puzzlement
    as I key in, again, the alarm's code to disarm
        while triggered floodlights flash in the hall,

and recorded hounds bark at my back,
    a bit overkill, I know, my neighbor said
        when we spoke earlier this evening by phone,

this grandfather whom I've seen return
    fallen eggs to their nests, one hand cupped
        and held out as he climbed the ladder,

his face rising and setting over the limb,
    I imagined, like the sun on the bayou to the west
        of our homes, my neighbor a retired internist

who for decades considered how organs
            interlink in the body's dark caverns,
                        who shyly brought me medical journals

he'd saved, *something useful, maybe,*
            for your students, he said, *something*
                        about which to write, and though I couldn't

make heads or tails of the texts, I appreciated
            the gesture, his instincts on subject matter
                        and the interrelation of systems and art,

which brings me back to his request
            on the phone, that I inspect, each time,
                        every room of his house, the alarm service

detecting a fire, most likely a glitch,
            though one never knows, and I pass again
                        from room to room, placing my hand

on the doors, testing for warmth
            as I was taught as a child, each doorknob
                        cold to the touch, *like the hands of the dead,*

I can't help but think, around me the mechanized
            dogs refusing to heel, the dogs not immortal,
                        of course, but reflexive, residual, having no

will of their own, no attentive master,
            only design, like the stories of planes
                        that continue their course after cabin

pressure has somehow been breached,
      like ghost ships rising out of the fog,
            or clock chimes winding down in the night,

and, of course and again, there is no fire,
      the dogs only calmed when I reenter the night,
            click once more the deadbolt closed,

and step back into the street and my yard,
      my form held again in the light of the moon,
            its brilliance less than the scorch of the sun,

solitary, unlike somewhere tonight that new groom
      and bride, *given away* as in the turn of phrase,
            walking hand in hand on a distant beach,

all futures before them, their pasts behind,
      and the only sound the churn of waves
            as the sea smooths their steps from the sand.

JOINED TO ALL THE LIVING
THERE IS HOPE

"It was a sign, not just of the times
        but of optimism," the realtor said,
                pointing to my soon-to-be-home's "Nutone"

radio-intercom, its vacuum tubes humming
        as I turned the dial, the system original
                to the home's build in 1963, complete

with an atomic symbol of two electrons
        swirling an absent nucleus etched
                into the wall-mounted, rose-aluminum casing,

my wife, eight months pregnant
        with our second child, rubbing her belly
                like a crystal ball and surveying

the room's faux-wood paneling,
        the steel hurricane shutters covering
                the lone window and sliding glass doors,

my wife, I was certain, not thinking of the race
        to the moon but of the starter home
                we had outgrown, our clothes

on rolling hanger racks in the hall
        where boxes fell from closet shelves
                every time someone closed a door

or our daughter, on waking, kicked the sides
        of her crib, which is not to say, as new parents,
                that we weren't optimistic, my wife and I committed,

as Kennedy had said in his address at Rice
        (my wife and I had watched the video
                separately and at different times in different schools),

of his and the country's desire to pursue
        hard things "not because they are easy,
                but because they are hard," the address given

in 1962, fourteen months before Kennedy's death,
        more than a decade before I was born,
                my mother and father both seniors in high school

when Kennedy was killed, my mother at Paschal
        in Ft. Worth, remembering students skipping
                school to hear him speak that final morning

at his presidential breakfast at the Hotel Texas,
        over two thousand people attending, one photograph
                in my mother's yearbook showing Kennedy

in his dark suit, seemingly stoic on the hotel steps,
        his hands behind his back, chin raised,
                eyes toward the horizon and, it would be tempting

to interpret in retrospect, the future,
>> if not for the other photographs on the page,
>>>> one showing him at the podium, the camera

catching him turned and smiling to Jackie,
>> another showing Jackie at ease,
>>>> leaning forward in the convertible

as they depart, Kennedy resting one arm
>> behind her, the other extended along the top
>>>> of the passenger door as if it were the rail

of his wooden speedboat RESTOFUS
>> in Hyannis Port, the name a play
>>>> on TENOFUS, his father Patrick's boat

and the number of their family at the time,
>> the fact of the Kennedy family being both like
>>>> and not like the "rest of us" not lost

on anyone then or now, which, of course,
>> was part of their appeal, or at least
>>>> their image, the family playing football

on the White House grass, the spreads in *Life,*
>> images like Caroline's pony Macaroni pulling
>>>> Caroline and her mother in a sleigh

across the snow-covered lawn, Jackie aware,
>> always it seemed, of the ephemeral
>>>> nature of time, calling a reporter from *Life*

in the days after her husband's death to tell
        the reporter she had something she wanted
                to say to the country, the reporter driving

through a snow squall, the magazine about to go
        to press, costing $30,000 an hour to keep it
                on hold, though worth it, the editor believed,

Jackie telling the reporter, alone,
        that she didn't want her husband
                to be forgotten, didn't want the *person*

of her husband to be forgotten, separate
        from the recitation of his achievements
                or failures, how she had been repeating over

and over in the days since his death
        the "one brief shining moment..." line
                from the musical *Camelot*, the record

her husband often played at night,
        a point she made certain the reporter
                understood, how, though great presidents

would come and go, nothing could remain
        the same, a personal point for her beyond politics,
                just as she had refused to change her clothes

after the assassination, standing beside LBJ
        when he was sworn in on Air Force One,
                her husband's blood still visible on her pink suit,

Jackie saying prior to exiting the plane,
      Let them see what they have done, reminiscent,
           I cannot help but think, of Mamie Till-Mobley saying,

Let the people see what they did to my boy,
      following the murder of her son in 1955,
           the March on Washington taking place

eight years to the day after Emmett Till's murder,
      two months after Kennedy introduced
           what would become the Civil Rights Act,

President Johnson saying privately
      following its passage in 1964 that his party
           "may have lost the South for a generation,"

though also saying to the nation, "Until justice
      is blind to color…emancipation will be a proclamation
           but not a fact," emphasizing that the struggle

must be an unceasing one, just as Jackie
      had instructed to have an eternal flame
           installed beside her husband's grave,

the flame still burning almost sixty years
      since Kennedy's death, almost thirty
           since Jackie passed in her sleep in her Manhattan

apartment, "surrounded," John Kennedy Jr. said,
      "by the people and the things that she loved,"
           and even now when I cannot sleep,

or I come home late after teaching a class,
       my children and wife already in bed,
              I find myself, too, checking on those I love,

room by room, the ease of their sleep
       filling the house as I test again,
              out of habit, the locks on the front

and sliding glass doors, though nothing
       has ever threatened us here, the closest
              occurrence being on the week we moved in,

a man and his girlfriend abandoning
       their car on a nearby boulevard,
              fleeing the police after robbing banks

and convenient stores over a two-week span
       in neighboring states, the fugitives desperate,
              hopping fences, having evaded, momentarily,

the police in pursuit, all of which at the time
       I was not aware, patrol cars revving
              through the blocks, their lights flashing

as I walked dumbly out into the yard,
       just to see, I thought, until a neighbor,
              peering out from behind his front door,

silently shooed me back inside,
       where I locked the door, learning later
              that night from my wife as she refreshed

a newsfeed online that the fugitives
        had entered a neighborhood home,
                the boyfriend raising a pistol on

the other side of the glass of a patio door,
        pointing the barrel at the father
                who let them in, and I do not know

if I would have done as the father did
        or would have had any other choice,
                the parents' minds flashing, I imagine,

like the lightning that arrived that night,
        the percussive rain on their metal roof
                as they sat at gunpoint for hours, waiting

and waiting for something to change,
        scared, simultaneously, that it would
                or would not, their young daughter

asleep upstairs, the parents praying
        silently that the storm would not
                wake her, that it would muffle

the voices below, and when the fugitives
        did leave, fleeing in the family's car,
                the family safe behind, the mother

and father perhaps stared through the doorway
        into the wind and rain, the taillights
                of their car fading as if the house itself

had exhaled the fugitives into the night,
    or, more likely, the mother and father
        locked the door at once and hurried to call

the police to provide a description
    of their own car that, within the hour,
        was surrounded, ten miles away

on a dead-end road, the driver-side door
    open, behind which the boyfriend
        crouched, pinned down and firing

his pistol at the floodlights and squad cars,
    the bullhorn voices squawking like birds,
        though clearly not birds when the rifles

fired in a thunderclap and smoke
    curled in the dark from their muzzles,
        then silence, the tap of rain on the roof

of the car, a lone voice again on the bullhorn
    when the girlfriend crawled out
        from the backseat, her empty hands

shielding her eyes from the lights as officers
    rushed in like actors from the wings
        and cuffed her on the ground beside

the motionless body of her boyfriend,
    even the judge saying later at the girlfriend's trial,
        as reported in the paper, that it was impossible

to know if in that moment the girlfriend
        were accomplice or hostage, but what the judge
                did have was evidence, surveillance videos

from the robberies of the girlfriend in sunglasses
        behind the wheel, and, earlier, stuffing
                into plastic bags what money she could

from a cashier's drawer, facts, the judge said,
        that were "irrefutable," a word, to me,
                that conveys something both indisputably true

and beyond discussion, just as every intake
        of breath is a drawing inward and every exhalation
                is a letting go, a perpetual meditation,

as real as the voices that rise from the Nutone
        when I am unable to sleep, the system,
                these years later, I cannot bring myself

to remove, even as I search the dial for I know
        not what, the reception mostly static
                except for preachers imploring their flocks

that *man knoweth not his time,* or the announcers
        calling a ballgame somewhere in the night,
                the batter settling in at the plate as the pitcher

shakes off a sign and bears down from the mound,
        the moon again full just over his shoulder
                and round as the ball let loose from his hand.

A YEAR OF GROWTH

My youngest daughter does not know
    that each tree ring marks a year of growth
        when she selects a piece of scrap wood

from the sawdust and shavings
    that have covered our back patio
        and carries the board inside to color

the rings revealed by the saw blade,
    my daughter filling the arching semicircles
        until a rainbow appears as her sisters

lay other scraps across the floor to make
    a path on which to leap from board to board
        to furniture and back again in a game,

I imagine, every child in history has played,
    the game requiring only the belief
        that the ground is not as solid as it seems,

that a misstep or tip of balance will lead
    to peril, whether lava or river or canyon below,
        even though, while laughing, they jump again,

shrugging off each demise, protesting
   only when I collect the boards
     and insist that the world be ordered

over their appeals to fairness,
   the mantra of childhood, to which
     I and every parent I know responds,

Who says the world is fair? mostly resisting,
   though sometimes not, to itemize,
     while wielding a clothes-less Barbie

or broken toy like a judge's gavel,
   every slight from work and love
     and politics both foreign and domestic

as the neighbor's dog howls at the burgeoning
   moon and the kids give each other that look
     meaning, *What's got into Dad—all we meant*

was we were having fun? which is when
   I see myself reflected in the glass
     of the patio sliding doors and realize

how large I must seem to them,
   large, though clearly not authoritative,
     as the youngest starts spacing

the boards again behind my back,
   and I lift one and point to the rings
     in the grain and say, see, this too

was once alive, explain, though rooted,
>   how it turned its leaves to the warmth of the sun
>   and drew water from the earth, its limbs

not unlike yours when you lift the hems
>   of your skirts to hop through puddles
>   or wave to me from the treehouse

we are building together, a project begun
>   before the passing of their grandmother
>   though intersecting now with her loss

as grief permeates all things, and they ask
>   the questions one would expect
>   (if she looks down on them from above

just as they, from the tree, look down on me)
>   and the questions one doesn't expect
>   about how the tree feels holding

the remains of another tree in its limbs,
>   transformed, though it is, into a house,
>   and I tell them trees aren't capable

of abstract thought or have feelings
>   like we do, though what do I know,
>   thinking of Michelangelo's *Pietà*,

and Mary, though stone, holding
>   her deceased son, and how the body
>   is itself a house of memory and love

and loss, as my wife and I explained
          to our daughters, that the sadness they feel
                    is sadness, yes, but also love transformed,

that grief is love for the one who was lost,
          just as my wife expressed on the day
                    before her mother died, after a month

of hospice at her mother's home and the gift,
          my wife said, to be there with her,
                    to measure and administer the morphine

when the great pain came, when any touch,
          even a blanket, became unbearable,
                    to honor the effort at the end for her to stand,

holding to the walker, and request what would be
          her final bath, and my wife, afterward, drawing
                    a comb through the fineness of her mother's hair,

never more beautiful, my wife saying
          that night, and again the next day,
                    even after the workers had come so quickly

to take her, to gather and remove
          any remaining meds, count every pill
                    as her final breath still hung in the air,

and our daughters cried unceasingly
          so that when, that night, we drove away,
                    the trees that lined the road seemed to bow

to the car, to lift their limbs in the breeze,
>   the undersides of their leaves lighter
>>   than the backs, like the palms of hands,

which, I believed, if they could,
>   they would place on our car, on the shoulders
>>   of my wife, or interweave their limbs

as a canopy above us, their petals
>   below, and the road would no longer
>>   be a road but a tunnel, to where it ascended

I did not know, only that we were
>   like breath released at last from the throat,
>>   becoming the words we were unable to say.

IV.

THE BIRTH OF VENUS

There are no spokes beneath the sulfuric clouds of Venus
   despite what Percival Lowell—brother of the poet Amy

and descendent of the Boston Brahmin Lowells—believed,
   having observed at low aperture from his observatory

in Flagstaff, Arizona, spokes from a central dark spot
   on the planet's surface, Percival unaware in 1894

that what he saw was a projection of the blood vessels
   of his own eye, shadows from his retina overlayed

on the image of Venus, this self-deception reminding me
   of Chico Marx, disguised as Groucho in *Duck Soup*,

saying to the befuddled Mrs. Teasdale in a bedroom suite,
   "Who ya gonna believe—me or your own eyes?"

the joke landing because of its absurdity, the obvious
   switch of Chico for Groucho, only similar in nightcap

and cigar, the joke no less absurd than the movie's conceit
   of Groucho as the recently installed president and dictator

of the bankrupt country Freedonia to which Chico
     and Harpo are sent as counterrevolutionaries

from the neighboring Sylvania, all of this fictitious,
     of course, except for the movie's central critique

of the real-life warmongering and vanity of dictators,
     flaws different from Percival Lowell's quixotic belief,

his erroneous vision of Venus facilitated by the blood vessels
     of his own eye and the dark center of his optic nerve,

not a distant planet's raging storm but a conduit
     for the nervous system's lightning, Percival Lowell's legacy

existing mostly as metaphor for how one's undoing
     arises from within, most famously stated by Cassius

to Brutus, saying that "fault" resides "not in our stars,
     but in ourselves," a manipulative line intended to inspire

the murder of Caesar, though all three men die
     by the end of the play, a destiny no different for Percival Lowell,

buried in a mausoleum on Mars Hill near his observatory,
     and for Groucho, his columbarium niche flanked by cigars

and novelty masks at the Eden Memorial Park Cemetery
     in Mission Hills, California, only Venus persisting today

as both the still-shrouded planet and in Roman mythology,
     the goddess conceived when Titan Cronus,

at his mother Gaia's request, castrated Uranus, his father,
   with an adamantine sickle and flung the severed remains

into the foam of the sea from which Venus arose fully formed,
   depicted by Botticelli as adrift on a giant scallop shell,

the breath of Zephyr at her naked back and lifting her hair
   as she covers herself and waits to disembark,

to cinch around her the thrown floral robe, and stride,
   beyond all gaze, to the firmness of shore.

WHEN YOU LEAST EXPECT IT

After the photograph "House of Bears" by Dmitry Kokh

One polar bear, in a photograph of an abandoned meteorological station in the Russian Arctic, stares out through the frame of a glassless window, the building's interior dark as a Rembrandt painting, as another bear stands on the crumbling porch, his head lowered like an admonished dog or a bull contemplating a charge. Fog obscures the sun and sky like a theater scrim, and the bears almost appear to be sources of light in the photograph, their white fur gleaming, even though I know, despite being someone always late to the facts, to the news, that polar bear fur is colorless, that the bears' outer hairs are hollow and transparent, and that the hairs of the undercoat, though not hollow, are transparent as well. The bears reflect all light back to the viewer's eye, which makes their fur only *appear* to be white, though I imagine this fact is irrelevant to the photographer, leaning into his camera, the photographer who will say to a captive audience when presenting the images later, *Nature is always sending you something when you least expect it,* a statement, I imagine, irrelevant to the bears, who have no interest in sending anyone anything, except maybe more seal meat to their own stomachs, who, as long as I am imagining, are probably a bit peeved that their coats—designed to be, if not invisible, at least transparent—are rendered seen, the bears clearly preferring anonymity in these abandoned homes from which they have stepped. Of course, the bears are right to be suspicious as their sea ice retreats farther each year and rusted metal barrels that once held fuel litter their island like giant, discharged shotgun shells, as if the gun were as large as the boat on which the photographer and his team arrived, or as if the bears were themselves diminutive, each bear no larger than it was as a cub, born small enough to be held in one person's hand, born toothless and blind like all cubs, knowing only the scent of its mother, the mother having dug a den in autumn to give birth before nursing her newborns through winter. Consider her, thinned and tired, leading them out, nuzzling, clumsy all, up through the snow that has covered their den, emerging together, the mother's senses so honed that she can smell a seal below three feet of ice or on the surface some twenty miles away. Already the cubs bound and slide, testing the snow as she nudges them, as the artic sun spins in the sky. Soon enough, darkness will fall like the robes of a queen, and then, snout raised in the cross-cutting wind, she will teach her children to hunt and to feed.

PROXIMA CENTAURI

"A new world is unveiled every day," Étienne Klein,
a French scientist, posts online alongside an image
from the James Webb Telescope of Proxima Centauri,
the star nearest the Sun, 4.2 light years from Earth,
as he praises the image's detail revealing swirls larger
than the storms of Jupiter, a surface of churning flame
crimson as the blood that moves through his veins,
and space itself, dark as the chambers of a beating heart.
And who would not believe, or, at least, want to believe,
the telescope's gold-plated mirrors unfurling
in space like a monarch from its chrysalis,
like a dream itself, even when Klein admits
online that the image was not, truly,
of Proxima Centauri but of a slice of chorizo,
its backdrop not the abyss of space
but a square of cloth on his kitchen counter,
and admonishes his readers about cognitive bias,
claims to authority, and the diversions of "cocktail hour,"
stating that "no object related to Spanish charcuterie
exists anywhere else other than on Earth,"
which, though not his point, reminds me of the line
by Robert Frost that "Earth's the right place for love:
I don't know where it is likely to go better,"
the appeal of both embarking and coming back,

the boy climbing the birch tree until it could bear
no more and set him down again. Even William Shatner,
the actor sent to space on a billionaire's rocket, on a lark,
stared into the unblinking lens of the camera crew
upon return and, pointing to the sky, described
the moment of entering space, how, "in that big window,
it was only black and ominous, and that was death,
and this was life, and everything else just stood still
for a moment," describing himself as overwhelmed
with the sensation, Earth's preciousness a cliché,
he acknowledged, sure, but precious nonetheless,
while he also plugged his new album, at ninety, and a song
about lying in a field forty years ago and staring
at the moon and dreaming, always dreaming,
an actor known for his hokum, a cliché himself,
with videos of him reciting a beatnik version
of "Rocket Man" and starring in commercials
where he battles a karate team and catches blow darts
with his fingertips on behalf of a hotel reservation website.
Shatner appeals, of course, because he is in on the joke,
a winking self-awareness, inexplicable, clumsily sly,
as when he and Nichelle Nichols were required
in 1968 to shoot two versions of their kiss
as Kirk and Uhura, one on screen and one off,
and they intentionally flubbed their lines
in the offscreen takes, requiring CBS to broadcast
arguably the first interracial televised kiss,
a triumph of which they both spoke proudly
long after the series concluded, the series
virtually unwatchable from a contemporary
lens other than as an artifact of cultural modes,
its pacing and rhythms maddeningly slow,
Kirk's halting cadence as frustrating
as the sputter of progress itself, as all futures

unfurling their precarious arcs like the billionaire's rocket
or the USS *Enterprise* traversing, on wires,
a Paramount soundstage. "Space," Kirk repeats
in syndication, "the final frontier,"
then records the stardate into the captain's log,
a kind of space diary unlocked by his voice,
his tone unwavering as he stares
from the bridge into the starless dark
of the camera lens, of the future, and says,
"Warp speed, Mr. Sulu. Engage!"

THE STORM ON THE SEA OF GALILEE

When Rembrandt stood before the canvas that had been stretched
  across its wooden frame like a sail drawn taut in wind,
his paintbrush balanced in the crux between his forefinger and thumb
  like the boat's long rudder dipped into the Sea of Galilee,
perhaps, as art historians suggest, he contemplated faith and doubt,
  the frailty of both the body and belief, and painted fourteen men
inside the boat, Christ and the disciples, plus another man
  whom scholars believe to be Rembrandt himself in a cameo
of hubris or whimsy or fear, as light slashed through the clouds
  to illuminate the sea, and the sea rose up to eradicate the light,

Or instead of contemplation, like the two disciples leaning in
  to grasp Christ's robe, Rembrandt bent to his work
(scientists have analyzed Rembrandt's paint and found he mixed
  wheat flour into it as an agent that simultaneously thickened
the paint and made it more transparent), and when he placed
  the fourteen men, the squall that tilts the boat so that the hull
draws a line from the top left corner of the frame to the bottom right
  and the mast forms a perpendicular, intersecting line,
perhaps he thought only of particulars, the way one disciple hinges
  on the railing in the stern, one broad hand across his bald pate
as he either vomits his dinner over the rail, or stares down
  into the dark water, the grave from which he cannot be saved,
even by Christ who's two feet away, while in the bow of the boat,

another disciple, in full light, as if on the high end of a seesaw,
stares both heavenward and at the knot he's tying, which breaks loose
   as the sail bucks and slacks and fills, whipping in his hands,

And in the stern of the boat Christ looks startled, woken
   from sleep (in the Gospel of Mark, the disciples ask Christ,
"Master, carest thou not that we perish?" and Christ quiets the sea,
   saying, "Peace, be still," before admonishing the disciples—
"Why are ye so fearful? How is it that ye have no faith?"—which produces
   in the disciples, not an alleviation of fear, but fear transformed:
"And they feared exceedingly, and said one to another, 'What manner
   of man is this, that even the wind and the sea obey him?'"),
and the painting holds forever in this moment, the words unspoken
   on the lips of the disciples who reach for Christ's robe,
as the figure of Rembrandt (one hand grasping a rope, the other securing
   his hat to his head) looks, not at Christ, but out to the tip of the brush,
out to the painter, to the audiences that will appear over centuries,
   from Amsterdam, across Europe, over the sea itself—the painting
of the ship within an actual ship, roiling on the waves—until it is purchased
   in 1898, arriving in Boston in the collection of Mrs. Gardner
(whom the socialites call *Mrs. Jack, Belle, Donna Isabella, Isabella of Boston*),

While elsewhere in the country Henry Ford founds his motor company
and the Wright brothers take their first flight, and though women's suffrage
   is a decade away, Isabella amasses her collection and opens in 1903
(her husband died in 1898) a museum, fashioned on the palaces of Venice,
   three floors of galleries surrounding an interior, glass-roofed garden,
through which she strolls, imagining her son alive again and appearing
   before her, the sound of his footsteps on the stone tiles rising
like the patter of water down a fountain (her biographers claim that the loss
   of her two-year-old son, Jackie, from pneumonia was the animating force
behind her collection—unable to have another child, she saw art
   and its creators as her family), and so the painting remained,
Rembrandt, the disciples, and Christ, on the wall of the Dutch Room,

even after her death, through the First and Second World Wars,
through the Space Race and televisions opening like Cyclopsian eyes
   in every home, through assassinations of leaders, activists, and a president,
each speech played back again and again as if to call them from their graves,
as incantations, through helicopters lifting off fields in Vietnam,
the *thwonk-thwonk-thwonk* of the blades like mechanized,
   industrial hearts, through the fall of the Berlin Wall, through The Gipper,
through the hemorrhaging of the Exxon Valdez, darkening the waters
   of Prince William Sound to the color of the sea in Rembrandt's painting,
to the color of a purpling bruise, of blood dark within the body,

   As, in the boat, Rembrandt never releases the rope in one hand
or his hat in the other while gazing out into the museum, the world beyond
   its walls known only through impression (the sound of rain on the glass roof,
a muffled car horn, a St. Patrick's Day parade fading in the distance, even light
   itself tracing the same path each day across the floor), yet the world is fact,
not impression, and, as if in proof, two police officers appear at the door
of the museum on the night of March 18, 1990, one officer tapping
on the security door with a nightstick as the other, speaking
   into an intercom box, explains to the guard inside that the officers
are responding to a call, and when the guard releases the door (the buzz
   and click of the lock that lets them in—such small sounds,
sounds the thieves had likely heard hundreds of times before when entering
   an apartment building or bank—become the sounds the thieves
remember most, as if something unclasps in their chests, as if the world
   shudders in sleep and realigns), the officers explain to the guard
that they have a warrant for his arrest, and when he calls the other guard
   to the front of the museum, the thieves cuff both guards
and lead them to the basement, secure them to pipes and duct tape
   the guards' hands, feet, and heads, and though there are many
questions here ("What made the guard believe?" "Was there actually a warrant
   for his arrest—either coincidentally guessed or known of by the thieves?"
"Did his finger hover over the buzzer as he remembered his boss's instructions
   never to open the door, remembered his boss standing too close,

his boss's bad breath like the first thaw of spring when the garbage
   that has been frozen in the ice and snow blooms in the gutters
and subway lines of Sullivan Square, of Charlestown?"), the central question,
   the withering one, of "When did the guards first understand?" coincides,
perhaps, with the click of the cuffs around the wrists of the second guard,

   And what settles over the guards, bound in the basement,
when they are left through the night, separated forty feet from each other,
   each man hearing the other guard moving, trying to speak,
the muffled sound like a voice on the other side of an apartment wall,
   though a voice nonetheless, each man imagining his family at home,
each man's wife running between her children and the phone, attempting
   to comfort her children, though she cannot conceal her fear,
which appears to the children as anger, confusion, and their whimpers
   become full-throated cries as each wife bangs the phone against its receiver,
unable to hear, each wife talking to the other, each one's fear fueling the other,
   or perhaps neither of the men has a family, which explains
why no one arrives until the next morning, that both of the men,
   like monks or prisoners, like the disciples themselves, turn inward,
that the darkness forced upon them is clarifying, that, like Christ in the Garden
   of Gethsemane (the Apostle Luke describes Christ as praying earnestly,
his sweat "like drops of blood falling to the ground"), they see the future,
   the wrath that will befall them for allowing in the thieves,

While in the body of the museum, the thieves move quickly,
   both men producing box cutters from their pockets, one man cutting
The Storm on the Sea of Galilee from its frame as the other man draws
   his blade around the edge of Vermeer's The Concert
(in the painting, a man sits in a chair, his face unseen, his back to the painter,
   to the thieves, the man's broad shoulders and dark hair
dominating the two female musicians—are they his students, his daughters,
   strangers to him, to each other?—as one woman leans over the keyboard
of a harpsichord and the other woman, standing, lifts her right hand
   as if a small bird might land on the branch of her finger just

as she begins to sing), and the sound of the blades through canvas
     is not like a surgeon's scalpel parting flesh, but coarse,
like the sail writhing in the disciple's hands, or the curtain of the temple
     tearing from top to bottom at the moment of Christ's death,

And when the thieves roll up the canvases and drawings,
     the paint perhaps fissuring like Italian frescos, as the hull
of the boat on the Sea of Galilee splinters and one thief yells to the other
     that it is time to go, and they secure the rolls either by binding them
or placing them in tubes, and then as quickly as the thieves came, they are gone,
     these two police officers disappearing into the streets, perhaps throwing
     the works into a waiting car before speeding off into the night, or hustling
     over the uneven bricks of the sidewalk, shouldering past a woman
outside the museum, the two thieves brusque, unapologetic, as she curses them
     under her breath, then pushes them from her mind until the next day
when the guards are found, and she sees the robbery on the news,
     tries to remember the two thieves' faces, but only sees the men
as her two brothers, both dead for twenty years, her brothers, one good
     and one bad, as her father had always said, an obvious oversimplification,
but a distinction nonetheless, her father refusing to visit the older brother
     even the first time her older brother was arrested, drunk,
having punched a cop outside a bar in Dorchester, the cop a childhood neighbor
     whose advances she had spurned years before, calling her older brother
to liberate her from the date, which was why the cop had goaded her brother
     into the fight, though her older brother never needed much coaxing to fight,
or, for that matter, to steal, whether cars or drugs or other men's wives,

And as the evening news reveals the images of the stolen works of art,
the woman diminishes the volume, sits at her kitchen table and looks out
     to the Charles River, a small sliver of which she can see
from her fifth-floor walkup, the river by which her younger brother died,
     a heart attack while jogging, how she had been with him, a few steps
behind when his words had broken off midsentence, making a small sound
     that she remembers as a fluttering of breath, before he slowed

to a walk, then dropped to his knees, and though both of her brothers
  have been dead for twenty years (her older brother died
in a car accident two weeks after she passed the bar exam), her memory
  of them grows stronger, or perhaps her memory has recreated them,
replaced them, become its own form of faith, the way she catches
  herself at times almost calling a defendant or another lawyer
by a brother's name, how some slight gesture will make
  her long-dead brothers bloom in the bodies of strangers
and friends, her brothers' names on her lips as she places her hand
  lightly on a desk to steady herself, as the courtroom stills,
as the jurors settle into their small boat, and from within his dark robes,
  the judge brings his gavel down to commence the next trial.

V.

THE LETTING DOWN

There is an hour each evening not long after the sun
  has descended beyond the bay—the sliver of which is visible

from our front lawn—when my wife, wearing only a silk robe,
  having bathed and nursed our soon-to-be-year-old daughter,

delivers her on the cusp of sleep into the singularity of my care,
  the wisps of my daughter's dark locks still damp from the bath

and slick as the day of her birth, smoothed across her brow,
  behind her ears, and when I lower her in her stroller down

the steps from our door to the sidewalk, the stroller jostling
  at each small descent, I am reminded of the dolly, stacked

with boxes and books, that I trudged up and down flights
  of stairs, moving into or out of apartments and flats

during what passed for spring in those dying cities
  of Central New York, their money from salt or soda ash

long dry, where the sun went down by three in the afternoon
  and residents retired to a neighborhood bar converted

from a funeral parlor or Masonic Lodge, though tonight,
 as I guide my daughter's small carriage—

a strange contrivance: one part mountain bike,
 one part Victorian coach—instead of stepping out

onto black ice or sludge, navigating canopies of trees
 like tunnels of snow, or snowdrifts plowed and packed

smooth as plaster walls, I descend into the heat
 of a Northwest Florida summer, "Baja Alabama,"

the "Redneck Riviera," my glasses fogging over even at night,
 like sea glass churned onto the white sand beaches

or the frosted mugs the patrons raise at the Flora-Bama Lounge
 and Package, the bar straddling the state line, a house divided,

one spouse for Seminoles, one spouse for Crimson Tide,
 yet the walk will help my daughter sleep, the "letting down,"

a phrase our parenting tome employs to describe both
 the transformation of the body for nursing and a calming

routine at the end of the day, a phrase, to me, that implies
 not just descent, but surrender, the top of my daughter's head,

the tip of her nose, visible through the small window
 in the stroller's canopy, its nylon flap flipped back

like the dark cloth of an antique camera, the diminutive
 dictator, miniscule queen (her four teeth, two top

and two bottom, "like a piranha" my wife will exclaim
   not fully in jest) chirping now, singing out into the night,

practicing her sounds, her first words, the "Ma-Ma-Ma"
   she sends out like a sonar pulse or the staccato "Da-Da"

that references me, the dog, the coffee table, and a lamp,
   and though the parenting tome does not say what is circling

in her mind, I imagine her impulses not far from my own,
   the directives of eating and sleep, of laughter

and sorrow and joy, that she is Siddhartha tonight,
   a being solely concerned with the present, awakened

to the immediate world, so much so that I draw back
   the canopy, and she points to the moon and says, "This,"

then at the branches of the live oaks intertwined above us,
   Spanish moss draped in their limbs, and says again, "This,"

then back to mark me as "This" as well, her finger waggling
   as she laughs, a game we play where I pretend

to bite it as she draws it in, and though I am not naïve
   to the Buddha's claim that attachment is the root

of all suffering, which is another way of saying what all bluesmen
   sing, that each step my daughter takes is a step away,

a preparation, a rehearsal daily for when she must cast
   her mother and me adrift, whether she will see us

to the banks of the River Styx or release us in a funeral pyre,
  if not from a Scandinavian shore, perhaps into the Escambia Bay

as fishermen look on from their pontoon boats and catamarans,
  and their children launch bottle rockets towards Odin and Thor,

but that night, thankfully, is not tonight, and as I turn
  my daughter's stroller for home, it is I, for a moment,

who resemble the ferryman, and my wife, rubbing lotion
  down the length of her alabaster legs, is the ash tree,

the Norse goddess who lifts our daughter in sleep,
  her small form cradled and weightless in the boughs.

HOW TO FIGHT THE LION

"If you run, you will only die tired,"
the safari guide says to the tourists
jostling in an open-air Jeep that creaks
like a boat through the reeds and grasses.
The dirt path on which they drive is a river
cutting from left to right across my television
screen. "A lion, for short bursts, can out-
accelerate a gazelle, much less a human,"
he says, to which the tourists nod and hold
to the rail. "Imagine, as a rite of passage,
an adolescent boy having to kill a lion
not so long ago on these very plains,
the boy armed with only two items: a spear,"
the safari guide says, "and this…" producing
from his vest a stick approximately the length
of a fountain pen and sharpened to a point
on each end. Holding it between his forefinger
and thumb, the guide asks the tourists to guess
how the small stick might have been used.
"Stab at the lion's eyes?" a portly man,
sweating though his oversized shirt, says
while slicking back what remains of his hair
beneath a ball cap. "Stick him in the neck?"
a woman offers, raising her hand shyly

like a schoolgirl. "Throw it, and the lion
will chase after it?" a boy interjects
as his apparent brother rolls his eyes
and their mother tightens her grip on both
of their arms. "All of these are guesses, yes,"
the safari guide says, "but with each of these
choices, you still become dinner. Imagine,
instead, those teeth bearing down. Already,
the lion has surprised you, the pads of its paws
silent against the earth, the way it moves
like wind through the savanna's tall grass,
the lion's unimaginable patience, kneading
the ground, then its movement, faster
than thought, than instinct, its force against
you like the night itself turned to a storm,
an unseen wave crashing upon you.
Your spear is useless, its long blade abandoned
to the darkness, and your only way out
is through. Not much of a chance, but a chance
nonetheless," he says and makes a fist
around the shaft of the stick, the two sharpened
ends protruding from each side of his hand.
"Like this," he says, extending his arm.
"Into the lion's mouth, past the jaws
like a key into a lock, one end piercing
the roof of the lion's pink mouth, the other
into its rough tongue. It cannot eat
around what its mouth cannot close."
"Bullshit," a woman calls out in the Jeep.
At least I assume this is what she says,
the word bleeped by the show
as she describes the uselessness of the stick
against the lion's claws, how lions hunt
in packs, so, best-case scenario, even if
one lion were stopped, another, or more,

would quickly descend. "And what kind
of parent would send out their child?"
she asks. "And why only boys? What could
the killing of a lion possibly prove?
If the boy wants to document his manhood,
let him sit and braid his sister's hair
or comfort a sibling back to sleep."
My daughters, both now annoyed
by the show, by the lack of the lion itself,
demand I change the channel. The sole
reason they agreed to watch, to pause
on a non-cartoon, non-singing show,
was my promise of a lion, my younger
daughter making a small roar and raising
her hands like paws, my older daughter,
though having long abandoned
the imitation of animal sounds, still wanting
to see a lion spring from the grass
and charge the Jeep, paws rocking its metal frame.
Yet even as I relent, cycling the dial, searching
until my daughters insist I stop on a program
that repeats and repeats a song they already
sing all day, I want to protest that just because
the lion was not observed does not mean
it was not there, that even the thought of it
is a form of object permanence, one of the first
and most important stages through which
all humans progress, the knowledge
of presence, in absentia, of a doll, a parent,
or, in this case, a lion, which is a way also
of saying that nothing is new under the moon
or the sun, and that eyes in the darkness
are most often eyes, a shudder of reeds
not a trick of moonlight or shadow.

A SHORT CONCEIT FOR LOSS

There is a step a boxer takes, his right knee buckling
   as if the ring has tilted under him—a dance floor at sea

perhaps—that conveys so completely his surprise
   at the force of the blow passing through his body,

the air snatched from his chest before he can even
   call out, that he does not hear the referee's count,

or see his girlfriend or manager abandoning the stands,
   but instead only breathes, his cheek flush against

the canvas as if it were his mother's worried hand
   held, in a fevered dream, cool to the side of his face.

FOLLOWING MY DAUGHTER'S FITTING FOR A PROSTHETIC EYE

"I am fascinated by the beauty of sight,
but I never crave for it," a blind actor says,
brushing his fingers across the petals of flowers
in a softly lit bazaar. The camera tracks
from his hand to his grey-tinged hair
as a market breeze circles his linen shirt
and bamboo chimes patter the air.
Palm-size hollows of rain ripple
on the cobblestones, revealing there,
as the camera draws in, the digitized name
of the hotel in which my family and I
temporarily reside. The television loop
fades to black then starts again, resetting
the feed. Beyond the second-floor balcony,
I can see in the hotel pool my two daughters
and their mother—Margaret bobbing
in her chest-and-shoulder-strap floatation
vest (a device somehow come to be known
as a "puddle jumper" or a "splash jammer")
while Sibley clasps her hands above her head,
bends at the waist, and dives from the edge
of the board, disappearing beneath
the water then rising to the arms of my wife.
So the cycle goes—Sibley climbs the ladder

to dive again, and Margaret ambles
from the pool steps to the deck, darting
around the lip like a sandpiper.
In a moment, I will join them, as I have
so many times before, hotel after hotel,
either before or after a visit to a hospital
or doctor's office, their florescent-lit
or shades-drawn rooms—hollows
of time, of waiting—spaces as shuttered
as Margaret's sightless left eye,
stalking having grown in utero
throughout the vitreous, branching
there like a tree in perpetual night,
the eye's architecture impervious to any
window drawn with a surgeon's blade.
In Italian, the word "stanza" means
"room," and I often tell students
to think of a room when selecting
their words, that what is the body
but a collection of rooms? "Lamentable"
was a word one surgeon used regarding
Margaret's eye. "Irredeemable" was
another. So the cycle goes, not only for us,
but for the others as well—the young
couple whose sightless daughter wakes
at all hours, unaware of the transition
between day and night. *Three a.m., she stands
up in her crib and wants to play,* her mother
told us in the pastel halls of Bascom Palmer,
*and how can you hold it against her?
Last night we slept,* the father said,
*for five consecutive hours, the first time
in a year,* a slight catch in his voice
when he spoke, a quiver I have heard

in my own words as well, like a hairline
crack in good china, or ripples on the surface
of a pond. Researchers say that with no
knowledge of sight, a person who is born
blind does not dream in images,
but primarily in touch and sound.
I thought of this today as my wife and I sat
in our car following Margaret's fitting
for a prosthetic eye, both daughters asleep
in their car seats, our engine idling
as airplanes rose like glinting whales
above us from what seemed like just
beyond the other side of an unadorned park.
My wife photographed Margaret's eyelid
closed over the new prosthetic, the cellphone
snapshot a request from the ocularist to whose
office we returned when Margaret woke,
then back to the hotel where we are now.
As I have so many times before, I place
the palm of my hand over my left eye
and review the words I have written
on my laptop screen, then look out
to my family in the hotel pool.
I have done this when driving or reading,
when gauging a step from the curb—to try
to see as Margaret sees, and answer
the questions my wife and I have
about Margaret's perception of depth
or her field of vision, which is really
a question about the future, about what can
and cannot be foretold. I turn my head
and my family disappears into darkness
at the ridge of my nose—a mountain range
behind which they set. I turn back,

and they reappear. Our dreams,
those same researchers said, are a way
of rehearsing our fears, that we learn
from them the ways in which to persist
and prepare. So be it. We are most
alike in that darkness, waking in fear,
desperate for some calming touch,
for the voice that whispers, *I am here...*

VI.

HOW ONE CHOOSES TO SEE

1.

My wife calls to say my daughter's eye is out, initially suspected lost on the National Mall or in one of the museums that line the avenues named "Independence" or "Constitution," the eye, both unseeing and unseen, perhaps settled against the baseboard of a burnished terrazzo floor or come to rest at the feet of cavemen in a diorama.

2.

My wife knows, of course, that I know that when she says "eye," she does not mean the eye itself but the prosthetic, the shell made to resemble and cover my daughter's blind eye like one cupped hand resting upon another, the piece needed to fill the orbital space of the underdeveloped eye, and mimic, though imperfectly, the blind eye's movements, which in turn adhere to the attentions of the eye with sight, my daughter's right eye all-seeing like the one shared among the Graeae, the Grey Sisters, its return to them worth more, as the myth of Perseus unfolds, than winged sandals, Hades' Cap of Invisibility, an unbreakable sword and shield, and ultimately Medusa's snake-locked head coiled in an infinitely deep bag, her own eyes, though dead, still turning all who meet them to stone.

3.

Yet our daughter's eyepiece isn't lost, my wife says on the other end of the line, having found the prosthetic in the stroller, the piece gazing up at her from the folds of the blanket in which she had bundled our daughter against the unseasonable cold that has met us in Washington in March, our family—my wife and I and our two daughters—purchasing the tickets for the trip months ago, my travel for work, my wife and daughters free to explore, to climb marble step after marble step or stand at the iron fencing of the White House, as, we envisioned, my wife would point through the bars and say to our daughters that anything is possible, that a woman, just as they will one day grow to be, has become, for the first and hopefully not only time, the president of our country and its people.

4.

Imagine, less than a hundred years ago, she had planned to say, *that women could not vote.* No commercial airplanes flew in the sky. No televisions. No computers.

5.

Yet, of course, anything *is* possible, which is still the lesson to be learned, a cause for trepidation where there is hope, or, conversely, hope where there is trepidation, either choice dependent on how one chooses to see, which is also the reason my wife has called and I have slipped from the conference hall and into the street, tightening my scarf at my neck.

6.

Now found, the eyepiece must be reinserted, something my wife cannot do alone, especially with our older daughter in tow and the requirement that the eyepiece must first be cleaned and oiled then slipped, a sleight of hand, behind the eyelids, a suction cup (the device about the length of a pinky finger, second knuckle to nail) affixed to the eyepiece below the pupil, the almost imperceptible veining of the prosthetic having been painted with threads thinner than dental floss, a small heart hidden at the apex of the piece, drawn there to instruct her parents which end is up should the eyepiece rotate or be removed, the marking, for us, no less than a North Star above the fake pupil and iris, their illusions of depth fabricated by more than one thousand strokes from an ocularist's brush.

7.

The goal of the prosthetic, beyond medical necessity, is to achieve a graceful illusion, to be seen but unnoticed, to blend in, a great gift of which neither my wife nor I had been fully aware prior to the birth of our youngest daughter, our Margaret Katrina, sister of Sibley Rose, the blindness of Margaret's eye presenting itself at birth in the camera flash of the hospital photographer, her tentative knock on the frame of the open door of my wife's recovery room the morning after Margaret's birth, the photographer holding up her camera and brochure as my wife waved her in over my shrugging protestations.

8.

We will want these photos later, my wife had said, urging the photographer forward.

9.

Sight, too, requires passage, and what my wife and I did not know then was in the release of light from the photographer's flash how quickly that light would move, 300,000,000 meters per second, fast enough to travel from the Sun to the Earth in eight and a half minutes, substantially faster than the blink of an eye, a subject's red pupil manifested on film by light from the flash passing through the eye's vitreous then reflecting red to the camera off the blood-rich expanse of the retina.

10.

Yet if light cannot enter, it cannot reflect, causing, as in the photographs of our daughter, one pupil to present red, the other to present white.

11.

Some blockage there, a surgeon said to us a day later in his examination room, lights dimmed, the calmness of his concerned voice unnerving my wife and me most of all, the cataract of Margaret's lens impermeable as silt stirred in a reflecting pool into which one can divine no future.

12.

The hierarchy is life then limb, the surgeon said, for the sequence of what he, as a doctor, attempts to save.

13.

And if thy right eye offend thee, pluck it out, I thought, but did not say, the verse from the book of Matthew, the Sermon on the Mount, where Christ also admonishes his disciples not to worry, to take *no thought for the morrow, for the morrow shall take thought for the things of itself,* an impossibility then it seemed for my wife and me, still not much less of an impossibility now, I know, as I step from the curb to the crosswalk to the National Mall, my wife and daughters visible across that great field of our anxious nation, Whitman's words in my ear, *It avails not, time nor place—distance avails not.*

14.

My wife pushes the stroller with one hand, her other cupped around the prosthetic as Margaret and Sibley make chase like sparrows, tug at my wife's long coat.

15.

How unfazed they seem by the cold, laughing together, calling to me when I'm seen, their breath entwined on the air.

ABOUT THE AUTHOR

Jonathan Fink is Professor of Creative Writing at University of West Florida. He has published two previous books of poetry: *The Crossing* (Dzanc, 2015) and *Barbarossa: The German Invasion of the Soviet Union and the Siege of Leningrad* (Dzanc, 2016). He has also received the Editors' Prize in Poetry from *The Missouri Review*, the McGinnis-Ritchie Prize for Nonfiction/Essay from *Southwest Review*, the Porter Fleming Award in Poetry, and fellowships from the National Endowment for the Arts, Joshua Tree National Park, the Florida Division of Cultural Affairs, and Emory University, among other institutions. His poems and essays have appeared in *The New York Times Magazine, Poetry, Narrative, New England Review, TriQuarterly, The Southern Review, Virginia Quarterly Review, Slate,* and *Witness,* among other journals.

ACKNOWLEDGMENTS

Grateful acknowledgement is made to the following publications in which these poems, some in earlier versions or different forms, first appeared:

Armstrong Literary: "Cat on a Hot Tin Roof"
Autofocus: "The Prosperity Gospels"
Broad Street: "Gorbachev's Birthmark"
Cimarron Review: "A Short Conceit for Loss"
The Common: "Proxima Centauri"; "Following My Daughter's Fitting for a Prosthetic Eye"
Mississippi Review: "The Letting Down"
Narrative: "How One Chooses to See" (Under the title, "Washington, D.C. March 2017")
New England Review: "The Storm on the Sea of Galilee"
Nimrod International: "Leonardo's Mistake"
On the Seawall: "Don't Do It—We Love You, My Heart"
Parhelion Literary Magazine: "Something Useful"
Saw Palm: "How to Fight the Lion"
Shenandoah: "A Brief History of Execution"
The Southern Review: "Graves"
storySouth: "And Who Will Come for You?"
Terrain.org: "The Succession of Mothers"

World Literature Today: "Quinta del Sordo"

"Leonardo's Mistake" and "Don't Do It—We Love You, My Heart" were selected by Alan Shapiro for First Prize and Honorable Mention in Poetry, respectively, in the Porter Fleming Literary Competition, sponsored by the Morris Museum of Art. "Leonardo's Mistake" was also subsequently a semifinalist for the Pablo Neruda Prize and published by *Nimrod International.*

"When You Least Expect It" received honorable mention in the San Miguel Writers' Conference Poetry contest.

I am also grateful to the Sewanee Writers' Conference for a Mark Strand Scholarship, the Philosophical Society of Texas for their Award of Merit in Poetry, and the University of West Florida for its support while writing these poems.